Group Power I:

A Manager's Guide to Using Task-Force Meetings

William R. Daniels

University Associates, Inc.
8517 Production Avenue
San Diego, California 92121

Library of Congress Cataloging-in-Publication Data

Daniels, William R. (William Roy), 1941-
    Group power I: A manager's guide to using task-force meetings

    Bibliography: p.
    I. Communication in management. 2. Meetings.
3. Social groups. I. Title.
HD30.3.D34   1986   658.4'563   86-24955
ISBN 0-88390-032-7

Former Title: *Group Power: A Manager's Guide to Using Meetings*

Design & Layout: Carol Nolde and Ann Beaulieu
Cover Art: Rob Andreasen

PREFACE

The dynamics and procedures discussed in this book are geared specifically for task forces. A task force is a group that is formed solely to address a particular problem, decision, or plan. At the conclusion of its study and discussion, a task force traditionally presents its findings and recommendations to the organization and then disbands, having served its purpose. A task force is not responsible for implementing its recommendations; however, persons who serve on a task force often supervise the implementation of changes or decisions throughout the organization.

Task-force meetings are not the same as the regular meetings of a staff or project team. The "official" and political business of an organization is accomplished during regular meetings, which are action oriented. Task forces, on the other hand, discuss issues and make recommendations that are carried out during regular meetings. This book addresses the unique managerial needs of task forces. The companion volume, *Group Power II: A Manager's Guide to Conducting Regular Meetings,* published by University Associates in 1989, focuses on the managerial skills needed to conduct regular meetings.

The purpose of this book is:

1. To raise your consciousness of the potential of small groups as focal centers for intelligent coordination of the organization;
2. To provide a simple but functional concept of *the basics of group dynamics* so that you can check on the progress of a task force;
3. To suggest *procedures* that will assist your task force in achieving its intelligence potential;
4. To offer a series of *activities* that provide practice in the procedures suggested.

Although I am familiar with the huge amount of research that has been done on groups and their dynamics during the last thirty years, this book is not an effort to summarize that research. Instead, it offers a number of procedures that I have used with success and that seem effective with task forces. Although the study of small groups may be approaching a science, it is still a field for pragmatism for most managers. My advice to readers is to try it. If it works, do it some more; if it does not work, try something else.

Over the last seventeen years, I have seen these procedures work. I have seen managers with little confidence in themselves or their colleagues form task forces and, using these techniques, recover their self-respect and their sense of organizational mission.

I have seen managers who were once in a state of quiet panic use these task-force procedures sucessfully to confront overwhelming and hostile changes in their economic environments, design survival strategies, and move back to the offensive. I have seen successful groups use these procedures to revitalize their drive for excellence. And I have seen old and risky plans, backed by considerable organizational commitment, stopped in mid-stride by these task-force procedures, thereby preventing a "lemming-like" rush to the sea and destruction.

The task force has great potential as the focal center for cooperative thinking about an organization's problems and opportunities. The ability to develop and lead such groups has long been recognized as a characteristic of effective managers. To harness this potential, however, is not a matter of "natural leadership" or "charisma."

The ability to lead a task force comprises a set of skills that a manager must deliberately set out to acquire. This book outlines those skills, which are relatively simple. Part 1 of this book, The Basics, presents an overview of task-force dynamics. Part 2, Procedures, presents the above-mentioned procedures. Part 3, Activities, offers a series of activities that can be used to practice the procedures. Just as teams practice their plays in a low-risk setting before a game, you should use these activities in training before you use them at work. Training sessions will enable you to use the key procedures, and in many cases you will identify upcoming situations in which the practiced skills will be useful.

These procedures have worked for me in the past, and I'm confident they will work for you too. It may take a little time for you and your task force to become adept at using them, but you can expect the practice to begin paying off right away. You'll notice a higher level of group intelligence. Furthermore, your task forces will become energized and exciting!

William R. Daniels
Mill Valley, California

February, 1990

CONTENTS

Part 1:
The Basics

WHAT GROUPS DO BEST

The most common use of meetings is to bring people together to disseminate information. We can call this kind of meeting the *briefing*. Unfortunately, these meetings are never brief enough. The pure information dissemination meeting, held at regular periods during the work life of an organization, has one guaranteed result: boredom!

It is this experience of the regular staff briefing that has made most managers skeptical about the potential of groups. The briefing usually allows very little participation for most of the members of the group. The leaders of the briefing usually lack theatrical talent, so in a short period of time, the minds in the group wander. Out come the doodling pads and other distractions. By the end of the meeting, the subjects that have been talked about have been diminished in importance because they have been ignored.

Information is useless unless it compels people to solve a problem, make a decision, or devise a plan. Useless information bores people.

Most of us in an organization are bathed in useless information. If it were not for the trash can and cultivation of that state of mind known as blissful ignorance, none of us could survive. The regular staff briefing has not a chance when it is up against these survival instincts.

The first recommendation is to do everything possible to diminish the time spent in pure information dissemination. Getting people together solely for this purpose is to ask for failure.

The second recommendation is to give the group work to do. The underlying assumption in calling any good meeting is that people are being brought together to do what groups do best: employ their members' minds in processing information for the purpose of problem solving, decision making, or planning. Information processed for these purposes is useful—never boring—and the process of using it is one of discovery and exhilaration.

When possible, convert information sharing to problem solving, decision making, or planning. For instance, the announcement of a new policy can be a problem-solving agenda by presenting two or three cases to which the policy must be applied.

The appropriate work for which groups have an unusual capacity—problem solving, decision making, and planning—implies the following facts about an effective meeting:

1. An effective meeting is essentially an intellectual operation. The intent is to achieve a superior quality of thinking and understanding.
2. An effective meeting intends to bring together different minds in a variety of perspectives. Those who attend the meeting must be active.
3. An effective meeting is a working system that yields a product. These products are in the form of coherent analyses, solutions, decisions, and plans.[1]

Finally, if your problems, decisions, and plans are simple ones, do not waste other people's time by calling a meeting. Treat a group as a kind of superior intelligence, and engage the group in tasks worthy of it.

GROUP DYNAMICS

The issue of influence is the place to begin in order to understand the dynamics of groups. The influence structure—how power is distributed among the members—is the primary determinant of what is called the group's *norm state.* It will determine whose minds are used and how effectively they are permitted to function. These norm states are reflected in such things as who speaks first or who speaks last, whose opinion is accepted without question, whose opinion is always questioned, and whose opinion is generally ignored.

Formation of the norm state is a psychological priority for group members—the first thing that must be resolved. Unless a skilled leader controls our natural tendencies, most of us will spend a lot

---

[1]For research concerning what groups do best, the author recommends reading "Comparative Study of Individual, Majority, and Group Judgment," by D.C. Barnlund, 1959, *Journal of Abnormal and Social Psychology, 58,* pp. 55-60; *Small Group Decision Making* (2nd Ed.) (pp. 64-67) by B.A. Fisher, 1980, New York: McGraw-Hill; and *Group Dynamics: The Psychology of Small Group Behavior* (2nd Ed.) (p. 68) by M.E. Shaw, 1976, New York: McGraw-Hill.

of energy trying to get a position of advantage from which to influence the group. No matter what the stated agenda for the meeting
is, no matter what the task, we will first work on the issue of influence. We may appear to get right down to business, but, in fact,
we will be working on a "hidden agenda"—a contest to determine
a "pecking order" for the group.

There are many styles in this power play. Some are obviously
aggressive. Others wait for the aggressive members to exhaust one
another and then move in to take over. Some wait to see who wins
and then achieve status by making an alliance. There are those who
prefer the role of rebel. Others play the role of victim and manipulate
the group into rescuing them. We all participate—we are all in this
game and affected by its resolution.

We are affected because the "natural" resolution of the hidden
agenda usually leads to a norm state like that shown in Figure 1.
The rings should be interpreted as a topographical map. The top
of the hill is the small, inner ring, and the other rings show lower
elevations going down to the base of the hill. The X's indicate the
location of the group's members in terms of influence. The higher
they are on the hill, the more influence they have in the group's norm
state.

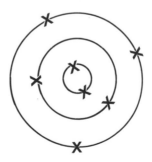

**Figure 1. Norm State After "Natural" Resolution of the Hidden
Agenda**

There are two problems with this natural resolution of the group's influence contest:

1. Although the group's members were called together to use all of the minds, this configuration will only permit the group to benefit from the minds of the dominant;
2. Even those who constitute the ruling minority will be less effective: they must think defensively because those on the "outside" become critical spectators; they think like grumbling outcasts.

With this sort of norm state, the meeting is never safe enough to allow any of its members to risk being imaginative or creative. The resources of the membership are therefore lost in two ways: some members do not get to say much at all, and those who do talk are so careful that innovative, interactive thinking does not occur.

Unfortunately, once a norm state is formed, even an ineffective one, it has great staying power. All the members of the group tend to rationalize their roles and enforce the current norm state.

For instance, you can ask a dominant member of an ineffective group, "Don't you think it would be a good idea to get some of the quiet members to talk more?" Often the response is "They're adults. If they have something to say, let *them* take responsibility for saying it." And you can ask a quiet member, "Why don't you say more?" In this case a typical response is "The meetings are such a joke that I don't want any part of them."

A group's tendency to maintain its norm state and to defend it against change can work to the group's advantage if that norm state is an effective one. The ideal norm state is one in which all members of the group have equal influence (Figure 2).

Here, all members are on the same level. Even the leader will be on this same ring, though he or she has the unique responsibility of getting and keeping group members on equal footing. (This is the *maintenance objective* of group leadership and is also the responsibility of every member of the group.)

When this norm state of equality exists in the group, information flows among all of the members with greater ease, and each member is freer to process that information for the group's intended purpose. Each member gives other ideas a serious hearing and feels both the right and the obligation to share relevant information and interpretations. This exchange is essentially a rational process, though its intensity invariably arouses feelings. But through it all,

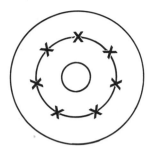

Figure 2. Norm State When All Members Have Equal Influence

each member retains the right and the obligation to stay in the process and sustains the respect of the other group members by fulfilling his or her part of the group's work. Because every member contributes to the group's efforts, the final product is one that recognizes every member's perspective. Through this norm state, the group utilizes all of its resources in the accomplishment of its task.

The greatest opportunity to affect norm states is during the first few minutes of the meeting. This is the time when all the members' nervous systems are most compulsively engaged in the influence contest. As was stated earlier, this is usually a covert process. Beneath the appearance of getting oriented to our task, and largely at the nonverbal level, each of us is processing millions of bits of sensory data to understand and establish ourselves in the group's influence structure.

This preoccupation of the members' nervous systems provides the effective group leader with a unique opportunity to control the formation of the group's norm state. The leader uses a method called *inclusion activity*. It consists of having everyone act pretty much like everyone else for these first few minutes. Everyone sits in the same kind of chair, with an equal view of everyone else. Everyone takes a brief turn talking, for an equal period of time. *What* people say is not so important at this point as *how* they say it—the uniformity of their behavior is the real message.

Uniformity of behavior in the first few minutes increases the probability that the group will resolve the influence and membership agendas in favor of a norm state of equality. Once the norm state is in place, the group will defend and maintain it just as it does any other norm state. But now the members' efforts will be on behalf of the group's intellectual success!

Groups may have real problems, but they also have real promise. You can avoid the problems and achieve the promise by establishing and maintaining a norm state that gives every member equal potential to influence the group. The procedures recommended in this book are all focused on contributing to the creation and maintenance of this kind of norm state.[2]

BASIC GROUP PROCESS

For a group to engage its tasks in an orderly fashion, it has to proceed through three stages:

1. Building the information base;
2. Analyzing the information base;
3. Resolution—arriving at a group decision or common agreement about the meaning of the group's information.[3]

Unskilled and poorly led groups attempt to do all three of these stages at once. Mixing the stages leads to confusion and inferior group work. Building the information base is inhibited and distorted by premature evaluation and decision making. Frustration and conflict grow as the group members find themselves necessarily repeating information and arguing from uninformed positions.

---

[2]For a general discussion of inclusion needs, read *Process Consultation: Its Role in Organization Development* (pp. 31-38) by E.H. Schein, 1969, Reading, MA: Addison-Wesley, and *The Dynamics of Discussion: Communication in Small Groups* (2nd Ed.) (p. 461) by S.E. Jones, D.C. Barnlund, and F.S. Haiman, 1980, New York: Harper & Row.

[3]These three stages are presented in "Phases in Group Problem Solving" by R.F. Bales and F.L. Strodtbeck, 1951, *Journal of Abnormal and Social Psychology, 46,* pp. 485-495.

To progress in an orderly way through these stages, a group must abide by certain procedures. This orderly handling of information is the objective of all group procedures.

A skilled, well-led group approaches its task by first making sure to collect all available facts, i.e., all of the information available from its member sources. This information base is built without analysis, though some discussion for purposes of clarification and elaboration may take place. Only when the information base is understood and complete will the group move to a period of analyzing the information.

The analysis of the information requires the members to express their opinions. Their analysis progresses in an orderly fashion because there is common agreement about the facts they are all interpreting. Usually, the analysis stage is characterized by the first signs of conflict. Such conflict is healthy as long as it remains faithful to the group members' information base. (If we had not wanted a variety of perspectives, we would not have invited a variety of people to the meeting.)

The skilled group moves to the resolution stage only when it is satisfied that the information base has been fully analyzed and that all relevant alternatives have been identified. Now the group seeks the agreement of its members. The resolution stage often causes the conflict level to reach a climax. The final agreement emerges as a reflection of both the information base and the thoroughness and variety of the participants' analysis.

The resolution may be the discovery of a problem's cause, a decision to move in a particular direction, or a complete action plan. Such resolutions, achieved by a group that has progressed in an orderly fashion through the three stages of its process, are usually superior in quality to the thinking of any individual member and are frequently implemented with greater commitment and efficiency.

GROUP DECISION MAKING AND ORGANIZATIONAL ACCOUNTABILITY

After the group has built its information base and has analyzed its information in Stages 1 and 2, it is ready to move into resolution,

Stage 3. Resolution will take one of two alternative forms: *consultative decision making* or *consensus decision making.*

Consultative Decision Making

A consultative decision-making process is one in which the members of the group have been asked to provide their information and interpretations, but *one member*—perhaps the leader—reserves the right to make the final decision. By using the group's resources, the deciding member enriches his or her own decision-making process. This is because the deciding member gets to hear the other members sharpen and elaborate their various positions through discussion with one another. Having each member consider his or her advice in light of all of the others' views usually gives the deciding member a much better information base and analysis than could be achieved by talking to each member alone.

At the resolution stage, the deciding member usually summarizes what he or she has heard and states the final decision. It is important for the deciding member to share this decision at the end of the meeting. Failure to do so leaves the group members uncertain of their value, perhaps invites bitter "politicking" after the meeting, and increases the possibility that a later announcement of the decision will be misunderstood. If, at the end of the meeting, the deciding member is not ready to decide, that should be said to the group. Ideally, the group should be reconvened later and should be the first to hear the decision.

Consensus Decision Making

A consensus decision-making process is one in which the resolution is achieved only when *all members* of the group agree that it is the best possible decision given their information base and its evaluation. Every member has the authority to veto the decision until, in fact, each member has found it possible to agree on a rational basis.

Consensus decision making leads to the highest-quality decision. But it is a process that always involves high levels of conflict and takes large amounts of time.

Consensus decision making probably should not be attempted unless all members of the group have been fully trained in group dynamics and are showing high levels of participant skills. It requires especially effective group leadership.

Some leaders attempt consensus decision making with the announcement that if consensus cannot be achieved within certain time limits, the leader will move to consultative decision making. This is a fundamental violation of consensus decision making. The superior work of the consensus process is only achieved under the pressures of having to reach a rational compromise of all participant positions. When the leader is standing by as an "escape valve," this pressure is lost, and so is the unique value of the process.

To maintain the integrity of the consensus decision-making process, the leader and members must engage the agenda with the understanding that the status quo will prevail until resolution is achieved or in the event that resolution cannot be achieved. The leader should select agendas that can afford such a consequence. There are many such agendas, but they fall in two domains: (1) the domain in which the status quo is a *tolerable* compromise of contending interests; (2) the domain of pure initiative, where no action is necessary but where there *are* opportunities—as in research and development efforts, for instance.

Voting

Voting is not a rational group-decision-making process. A vote is simply an expression of individual thinking and its collective force.

Discussion prior to voting should enrich the wisdom of the individual's choice. But with voting as the resolution act, prior discussion usually takes a form other than rational persuasion. Bargaining, negotiating, and intimidation—both overt and covert—are at least equally effective if not superior ways to win a vote.

In the political domain of a democratic society, voting is necessary. There is no rational resolution to the conflicts existing between constituencies in a complex and vital culture. Yet some decisiveness is required. Voting is a relatively peaceful way of resolving such political issues. Voting, however, should be restricted to such political domains and should not be relied on in rational group work.

Choosing and Announcing

Most organizations use the consultative decision-making process as their basic resolution method. It balances a concern for time with the enrichment of group intelligence.

Whatever the choice, consultative or consensus, it should be announced at the beginning of the meeting. Knowing how the agenda will be resolved affects the role of every participant in the process. Waiting until the resolution stage has been reached before determining how it will be achieved is too late! It always offends enough members of the group to assure resistance to implementation of the immediate decision and resistance to participation in future meetings.

Accountability—Realizing the Group's Decision

One member of the group must be made accountable to the organization for the decision. If this is not done, group work can lead to organizational confusion. This is especially important to remember when the consensus process has been used.

Participation in decision making must be separated from the issue of organizational accountability for the decision. Without one person's being accountable, a group produces an "orphan decision." Frequently, if the decision gets into trouble later on, no one in the group takes responsibility for it, each blaming it on "those other members in the group who decided that." To prevent this problem, a group should never adjourn until its resolution has been delegated, for purposes of organizational accountability, to one member.

THE PRIMARY RESPONSIBILITIES OF THE GROUP LEADER

There are five key areas for which the group leader is responsible:

1. Providing an agenda;
2. Structuring the participation;
3. Providing for an inclusion activity;
4. Selecting appropriate procedures;
5. Providing a memory system.

These five responsibilities are the primary duties that a leader must fulfill. They are the minimum for group leadership. When they are achieved, the meeting is set for success; failure to do any one of these five things greatly increases the group's probability of failure.

Certainly the leader also has a special responsibility for group maintenance, but so do the rest of the group members; the leader may need to remind them of this every now and then.

Responsibility 1: Provide an Agenda

The agenda should be published before the meeting, should be a guide to the individual members' preparation, and should be a working tool for the group once it has been assembled.[4]

A good agenda covers at least the following items:

1. Time and place of the meeting;
2. The subject to be discussed;
3. The desired results from the meeting;
4. The names of those who will be attending;
5. The name of the person who is leading the meeting.

A complete agenda also provides all of the information on the following check list:

---

[4]For an excellent discussion of meeting planning and the function of the agenda, see *How to Make Meetings Work* (4th Ed.) (pp. 201-211) by M. Doyle and D. Straus, 1984, New York: Berkley.

Check List: Creating an Agenda for an Effective Meeting

_____ Name of group

_____ Title of meeting

_____ Who is calling the meeting

_____ Date

_____ Starting time

_____ Ending time

_____ Place

_____ Agenda put out ahead of meeting (at least one day but not more than one week ahead of time, so it will be fresh in people's minds)

_____ Desired outcomes

_____ Meeting procedure (nominal group process, force field, matrix decision, Gantt planning, etc.)

_____ Decision-making method (consensus, consultative)

_____ Final decision maker (group, meeting leader, other)

_____ Preparation suggestions (background materials, materials to bring)

_____ Other notes to participants

People Attending:

_____ Leader/chairperson

_____ Group members

_____ Role assignments (subject matter experts, implementation specialist, recorder, facilitator of dynamics and process)

_____ Guest resource persons

Agenda Schedule:

_____ Sequence of items

_____ Person(s) responsible for each item

_____ Procedure (see Meeting procedure on the opposite page) for dealing with each item

_____ Time allocated for each item

Responsibility 2: Structure the Participation

The leader is responsible for seeing to it that everyone necessary to the decision is present and that nobody unnecessary to the decision is present. Anyone attending the meeting who is not necessarily involved in the subject has a high probability of being a "graphite rod": an element that will slow down the group's interactive process as graphite rods slow down a chain reaction in a nuclear reactor.

Do not hesitate to restructure the group for each agenda item. Some items really do not involve everyone, so try to structure the meetings so that people can come and go according to the relevance of their participation. If they know ahead of time that this restructuring will occur, it diminishes any sense of being "left out."

It is important to know ahead of time who will be responsible for the group's work as far as the rest of the organization is concerned. Who will be accountable? If the group is to select such a person during the meeting, the group should know that before the meeting.

The person accountable for the resolution ought to be one level higher in the organization than any other member of the group. This is not always necessary, but it has been found to clarify issues of accountability when organizations use small groups.

Finally, pay attention to the size of the group. The following facts should be kept in mind:

1. A group with five to nine members most frequently outperforms individuals; this size seems to provide the best mix of resources and interpersonal dynamics.

2. A group with fewer than five members often fails to outperform individuals; either there are too few perspectives to make any difference, or the group is too easily dominated by one member.

3. A group with more than nine members often fails to outperform individuals; perhaps it is difficult for everyone to participate, or perhaps we get "spectators" and "stage fright."

4. Generally, even-numbered groups (two, four, six, eight, etc.) have a tendency to break into two even subparts, and these subparts often get into conflict with one another.

Responsibility 3: Provide for an Inclusion Activity

Whatever is done during the first five minutes of a meeting establishes the norm state. The leader must carefully control this five-minute period. Providing an inclusion activity is the easiest and best way to deliberately shape the norm state into one of equal influence. This activity simply asks everyone to participate in a similar fashion during the first part of the meeting. Use an inclusion activity at every meeting.

Responsibility 4: Select Appropriate Procedures

For people to focus their intelligence on one subject, they must have a guiding procedure. The free-for-all discussion is often inefficient.

The leader of the meeting should therefore decide ahead of time what procedures the group should use to achieve its purposes for each agenda item. Once the group has been trained in the procedures, these procedures can simply be announced. Until then, the procedure may have to be explained before the group engages in a task.

To facilitate the leader's performance of this function, a number of appropriate procedures are suggested in Part 2 of this book.

Responsibility 5: Provide a Memory System

Group members do not think well together unless they have a common memory. A common memory is provided by making it possible for each member to see what ideas the group has already considered. The most common form of group memory system is the use of a flip chart and felt-tip markers.

The requirements for a good memory system are that it:

1. Be visible to all members of the group;
2. Be maintained simultaneously with the group's thought process;
3. Accurately reflect the *verbiage of the group members.*

The leader does not necessarily have to be the person who writes on the flip chart. This task may be delegated to a *recorder.* But the function is necessary. No matter how experienced group members are in working with one another, they never outgrow their need for a memory system. Smart group leaders know this, and they provide the mechanism without any opportunity for the group to ask questions about it.

After each session of a meeting, the charts are collected and saved for display at the beginning of the next session. It may be desirable to make a typed copy of the charts for each member. In this case, the charts are typed up in order of their creation in the meeting. (Number the charts as the meeting progresses.) Several charts will usually fit on a single page. A dotted line across the page can separate different charts.

Ask your secretary not to alter the charts. Psychologically, the members' memories are associated with the exact appearance of the charts, so the charts need to be copied as precisely as possible. Arrange words in relationship to one another as they appeared on the original charts and copy in by hand any diagrams or other artwork. These copies of the charts become the *working minutes* of the meeting. At a later time, the group may need to draft a final report for publication.

Summary

The problems groups have are often due to their dynamics and process rather than to their actual tasks. Typical problems include:

- Inadequate procedures;
- Hidden influence agendas;
- Various forms of group pressure on individuals (group blackmail).

The mark of a mature group leader is the ability to give simultaneous attention to the group's task (its quality of results), to its dynamics (its norm state), and to its process (its adherence to appropriate procedures). This multilevel listening is the most important skill for a leader to have.

An effective group leader responds to what is happening with appropriate suggestions, timely alterations in procedures, and occasional (but always tactful) confrontation.

GROUP PARTICIPANT RESPONSIBILITIES

For a group to achieve its potential, every member of the group must have certain minimal skill levels. Specifically, each member must be able to perform two types of participant functions: task-related functions and maintenance-related functions.[5] *Task-related functions* are what participants do to process the group's information in order to achieve its intellectual product. *Maintenance-related functions* are what participants do to help maintain the group's norm state of equality in influence.

There are seven basic task-related functions to be performed in groups.

1. *Initiating.* Someone should "get the ball rolling" by presenting the initial ideas with which the group is to interact. This initiation should occur both at the beginning of a meeting and at critical transitions as the group moves from one part of its thought processes to another. Initiation is often coupled with summary as a function.

2. *Providing Information and Opinions.* Every group participant should come prepared to provide relevant information and ideas for the meeting topic. Each should feel a sense of obligation to share.

3. *Asking for Information and Opinions.* Knowing what you do not know and what the group does not know is important. Members should be encouraged to point out omissions in the data base from which the group is operating by asking for that additional information.

4. *Clarifying.* Until the information has been presented in a way that is coherent and comprehensible, a member should keep working on the information. Restating it, questioning it, and testing it against hypothetical situations are all ways of clarifying it.

---

[5]The classification of role functions in a group was presented in "The Effects of Cooperation and Competition upon Group Process" by M. Deutsch, *Group Dynamics—Research and Theory* (2nd Ed.) by D. Cartwright and A. Zander (Eds.), 1960, Evanston, IL: Row Peterson. Also see "Functional Roles of Group Members" by K. Benne and P. Sheats, 1948, *Journal of Social Issues, 2*, pp. 42-47, and "A Set of Categories for the Analysis of Small Group Interaction" by R.F. Bales, 1950, *American Sociological Review, XV*, pp. 257-263.

5. *Elaborating.* Group participants should have the ability to see an idea's implications and ramifications and to point these out. This is the function of elaboration.

6. *Summarizing.* This task requires someone to state clearly where the group is in its procedures and information processing and to set out the next steps. Without frequent summarizing, groups lose their sense of direction.

7. *Compromising.* When different perspectives have been expressed and have been found to be in at least partial conflict, the group should make an effort to find a rational position that is faithful to both of the conflicting perspectives but that supersedes them in a unifying concept. Hammering out this unifying concept is the skill of compromising; it is an essentially rational function.

There are four basic maintenance-related functions to be performed in groups.

1. *Gatekeeping.* This is the function of one participant's inviting another to speak. It is a deliberate turning of attention to people who may need help getting a chance to speak; it is also a way to take attention away from someone who is talking too much.

2. *Harmonizing.* This function seeks to calm and to relieve people of distractive emotionality. When people fall away from rational argumentation and begin to indulge in intensive emotionality, it is important to "harmonize," to get people to recognize their feelings and the fact that the feelings are getting in the way of the group's information processing.

3. *Testing the Group's Norm State.* This is a dangerous function because groups are defensive about norm states. The task is a deliberate effort to focus the group's attention on a pattern of operation that is working against an equal-influence structure, and must therefore be performed tactfully.

4. *Encouraging.* This function is crucial to a group's morale. At times the group will become frustrated in its operation as it deals with a difficult problem without immediate success. At such times the function of encouragement helps a group recall past successes or helps it focus on the benefits of staying at the task at hand.

Part 2: Procedures

PREVIEWS

When to Use This Procedure

1. As an inclusion technique when working with a group in which the members are familiar with one another and with working together;

2. At the beginning of a meeting.

Materials Needed

None.

How to Use This Procedure

1. The leader asks each member of the group to express his or her tendency toward the first item on the agenda, giving a sixty-second time frame for the expression of this beginning position.

2. Each member of the group uses sixty seconds to state his or her basic opinion.

3. When all members have spoken, the leader briefly summarizes the basic positions that have been stated and uses that summary as the springboard from which to start work on the first agenda item.

PETER/PAUL[6]

When to Use This Procedure

1. As an inclusion technique when the members of the group do not know one another well or do not work with one another on a constant basis;

2. At the beginning of a meeting.

Materials Needed

1. Pencils, one for each group member.
2. Note pads, one for each group member.
3. A prepared list of questions posted on a flip chart (see Step 2).

How to Use This Procedure

1. The leader of the meeting says, "I think it would be a good idea for us to take a few minutes to meet one another before we get into today's agenda. I suggest you follow this procedure. Team up with one other person you are least acquainted with, and interview each other during the next five

---

6From "Peter-Paul: Getting Acquainted" by E.L. Solley in *The 1973 Annual Handbook for Group Facilitators* (pp. 7-8) by J.E. Jones and J.W. Pfeiffer (Eds.), 1973, San Diego, CA: University Associates. Adapted by permission.

minutes, getting the answers to these questions." (The leader displays the list on the flip chart.) "When the five-minute period is done, you should be prepared to introduce the other person and to give us this information."

2. Members of the group pair up and spend five minutes interviewing each other to get the answers to the questions posted on the flip chart. These questions might be:

- Name?
- Current position or title?
- Length of time in current position?
- Number of people managed?
- The parts you like best about that job?

Note: These questions can be altered depending on the members of the group and the purpose for which they are getting together. Keep the questions simple, basically positive in their focus, and low risk in terms of how much they require people to disclose of themselves.

3. When pairs have completed their interviews, the leader asks them to introduce each other in the following manner: "When you introduce each other, I'd like you to do it this way." (The leader models this behavior while describing it.) "Stand behind the person you are introducing, put your hands on his or her shoulders, and introduce him or her as though you were the person you are introducing. For instance, if I were introducing Mary, I would say, 'Good morning, I'm Mary; I currently hold such and such a position, etc.'" The pairs take turns introducing each other in this manner until all members of the group have been introduced.

 BRAINSTORMING[7]

When to Use This Procedure

1. When you want to generate a large quantity of information prior to problem solving, decision making, or planning;

2. When you want to inspire creativity in the group thought process.

Materials Needed

1. Flip chart (usually several sheets hung on the wall in preparation).

2. Markers.

How to Use This Procedure

1. The leader names the subject about which a variety of alternatives or ideas are desired and provides an allotted time for the brainstorming session.

2. The group generates as many ideas as possible, given the objective stated in Step 1. The emphasis is on pure quantity, so as fast as the ideas can be said, the recorder writes

---

[7]Brainstorming was introduced in *Applied Imagination: Principles and Procedures of Creative Problem Solving* (3rd Rev. Ed.) (p. 417) by A.F. Osborn, 1963, New York: Scribner.

them on the flip chart. (This may require more than one recorder working simultaneously.) The idea is to get everyone talking as rapidly as possible to generate a large volume of ideas.

Note: The basic rule is that no idea can be evaluated, judged, or criticized in any way. All ideas are accepted.

Note: It is fair to "tailgate" on other people's ideas, i.e., to elaborate on them with variations. Record all of these variations.

3. When the period of time for brainstorming has ended, the group evaluates the volume of ideas generated in Step 2. The members select from the list those ideas that they think are most worthy of further exploration and elaboration.

Note: The act of brainstorming simply separates two distinct intellectual functions—(1) quantitive generation of ideas and (2) evaluation of the quality of ideas. It has been found that creativity and quantity of ideas are most easily generated in an environment that is safe from evaluation or criticism. Once a large volume of raw ideas is available, the evaluative process will usually yield a higher-quality final decision.

NOMINAL GROUP PROCESS[8]

When to Use This Procedure

1. When you want to assure that individuals comprehend a problem before the group begins working on it;

2. When you are worried that people are failing to do their own thinking—that they are simply reacting to one or two other people's ideas;

3. When participation in the group's task has become unbalanced or has degenerated into an argument among two or three members—i.e., the nominal group process can be used to restore the group's norm state of equal participation and can broaden the information base to open avenues of compromise.

Materials Needed

1. Pencils, one for each group member.

2. Note pads, one for each group member.

---

[8]Based on "A Group Process Model for Problem Identification and Program Planning" by A.L. Debecq and A.H. Van de Ven, 1971, *Journal of Applied Behavioral Science, 7,* pp. 466-492, and on "Nominal Group Technique: An Applied Group Problem-Solving Activity" by D.L. Ford, Jr., in *The 1975 Annual Handbook for Group Facilitators* (pp. 35-36) by J.E. Jones and J.W. Pfeiffer (Eds.), 1975, San Diego, CA: University Associates. For a discussion of the nominal group process, see "Applied Group Problem Solving: The Nominal Group Technique" by D.L. Ford, Jr., and P.M. Nemiroff in *The 1975 Annual Handbook for Group Facilitators* (pp. 179-182).

3. Flip chart.

4. Markers.

How to Use This Procedure

1. The leader gives each member the problem agenda, i.e., the statement of the problem. The members individually write down their perceptions of that problem, perhaps within a time frame, paying attention to specific questions:

   • When does it happen?
   • To whom does it happen?
   • What is involved?
   • What is the problem's cause?

   (The leader can instead give this assignment to the members prior to their coming to the meeting.)

2. Each member reports his or her thoughts and facts within a given time frame, maybe five minutes or more. While each member reports, the other participants may only ask questions for clarification; they may not evaluate or elaborate on the ideas. If the ideas are not clearly understood, however, each participant is responsible for asking the questions necessary to assure his or her own understanding. A recorder charts each individual's information, or the individuals may do this for themselves as they make their presentations.

3. In subgroups or as a whole, the group takes the information that has been presented and does one of three things:

   • Makes a new summary list that includes all of the ideas but eliminates duplications;
   • Goes through all of the ideas that are there and selects those three or four that are the most worthy of the group's further exploration, i.e., *prioritizes* the ideas in terms of their significance;

- Explores patterns in the information: areas of general agreement, significant disagreements, major alternative perspectives of the problem, a *real-time* sequence of the facts, frequency of occurrence, etc.

4. The group seeks to define the problem with one statement that deals comprehensively with all of the information.

5. The group seeks to state the probable cause or causes of the problem. (The group can move at this point to any one of a number of problem-solving procedures.)

NOMINAL PRIORITIZATION

When to Use This Procedure

1. When you have a number of alternatives from which you have to select one;

2. When a simple method of prioritizing alternatives is suitable.

Materials Needed

1. Flip chart.

2. Markers, one for each group member.

How to Use This Procedure

1. The leader displays the list of alternatives so that all members of the group can see the entire list.

2. Each member of the group receives a marker. All members simultaneously go to the list; each puts a number 3 with his or her initials next to the item he or she considers to be most important, and a number 2 and a number 1 for the second and third most important items, respectively, initialing their numbers in each case. When this step is completed, each member will have selected the three most important items and will have expressed this selection. The

items with the highest total points are those considered most important by the group at this initial stage. (This is only voting, however, and if the leader stops the process at this point, no rational exchange of information will have occurred.)

3. In a limited period of time (two to five minutes) each member explains his or her selection of the most important item.

4. *Optional:* The leader may also want to give the members an opportunity to argue for their second and third choices.

5. On the basis of the information thus far processed, the members are allowed to alter their first selections (to express a new sense of priorities).

6. The group discusses the remaining disagreements, arriving at a final decision either by a consensus or a consultative method.

PROBLEM PROBE[9]

When to Use This Procedure

1. When you want to isolate precisely the cause of a problem;

2. When you have a significant problem that is worthy of detailed analysis to find its cause.

Materials Needed

1. Flip chart.

2. Markers.

How to Use This Procedure

1. The leader presents the group with the initial statement of the problem. This statement should cover what is currently happening contrasted with a statement of what should preferably happen. The gap between these two descriptions is the area of the problem.

2. The group provides information to answer the following questions:

---

[9]Used with permission. Kepner-Tregoe, Inc., an international organization based in Princeton, New Jersey, specializing in strategic and operational decision making; adapted from 44-47 of *The Rational Manager*, Copyright © 1965 by Charles H. Kepner and Benjamin B. Tregoe. All rights reserved.

- Where does the problem happen?
- When does the problem happen?
- What material or equipment is involved?
- Who is involved in the problem?
- What processes or procedures are involved?

3. The group provides information to answer these questions:
   - Where else could this problem be happening, but does not?
   - When could this problem be happening, but is not?
   - Where is the same material or equipment being used without this problem?
   - Who could be involved in the same sort of problem, but is not?
   - Where are the same processes or procedures being used without this problem?

4. The group reviews the data generated thus far and lists the characteristics that distinguish the items in Step 2 (factors involved in the problem) from the items in Step 3 (factors not involved in the problem). These distinctions define the domain of the problem. The cause of the problem operates only within this unique domain—within this special pattern of location, timing, resources, and procedures.

5. The group lists any changes that have been made that affected only the unique domain identified in Step 4, i.e., those changes affecting only the problem domain or affecting all other domains except that of the problem. The group looks especially for changes made or occurring just prior to, or near, the same time that the problem became noticeable. (Changes are a prime source of problems.)

6. Based on the information and analysis done so far, the group seeks to redefine its problem and to deduce its cause. The leader should test this cause as *the* cause by asking whether or not it works only in the problem's unique domain; the cause will not affect the domains where the problem could, but does not, exist.

Note: Groups using this procedure soon learn that it is important to provide information for all of the questions in Steps 2, 3, and 4. This may involve recessing to find the information. The procedure shows the group members where to focus their research. With that research, this is an extraordinarily powerful procedure for problem analysis.

DECISION MATRIX[10]

When to Use This Procedure

1. When you will consider several alternatives in the decision-making process;

2. When you feel that the decision deserves fairly elaborate attention.

Materials Needed

1. Flip chart.
2. Markers.

How to Use This Procedure

1. The group brainstorms a list of characteristics of an ideal solution, decision, or choice. All of these characteristics are charted.

2. The group evaluates the list of characteristics to see if any are "veto" characteristics; if an alternative decision or solution fails to have this characteristic, it will not be an acceptable alternative.

---

[10]Used with permission. Kepner-Tregoe, Inc., an international organization based in Princeton, New Jersey, specializing in strategic and operational decision making; adapted from 48-51 of *The Rational Manager*, Copyright © 1965 by Charles H. Kepner and Benjamin B. Tregoe. All rights reserved.

3. The group prioritizes the remaining characteristics into two classes: those that are "highly desirable" and those that are "also desirable."

4. The recorder arranges these ideal characteristics on the vertical axis of a matrix, placing the "veto" items at the top, then the "highly desirable" items, and finally the "also desirable" items at the bottom. (See Figure 3.)

5. The group lists, across the top of the matrix, all the alternatives worth considering in this particular situation. (In the Figure 3 example, the group was deciding which machine to purchase for a production business.) At this point it is good to push for creative thinking. The leader asks what new ways, other ways, or combinations and modifications of old ways might also fulfill at least some of the ideal characteristics listed in Step 4.

6. The group evaluates each possible alternative, one at a time, against each of the ideal characteristics on the vertical axis. Any time an alternative fails to meet one of the "veto" items, the group stops considering that alternative. For the "highly desirable" and "also desirable" characteristics, the group rates each alternative on a scale of one to five or one to ten in terms of how adequately it meets that characteristic.

7. For the "highly desirable" traits, the leader doubles the score given in Step 6, then adds the scores for each alternative. The highest-ranking score should be the most desirable choice.

Ideal Characteristics	Weight	Machine No. 1	Machine No. 2	Machine No. 3
Veto Characteristics				
Must meet OSHA regulations	veto	OK	OK	OK
Must produce 100 units/hr.	veto	OK	OK	OK
Must cost less than $65,000	veto	no	OK	OK
Highly Desirable				
Should have operational life of ten years	X2		5 / 10	5 / 10
Should have low maintenance needs	X2		4 / 8	5 / 10
Should require as little operator time as possible	X2		2 / 4	3 / 6
Should have high materials efficiency	X2		5 / 10	4 / 8
Also Desirable				
Should have efficient electrical power consumption	X1		4 / 4	5 / 5
Should represent state of the art for next five years	X1		5 / 5	4 / 4
Total Score	—	0	41	43

Figure 3. Decision Matrix Illustration

FORCE-FIELD STRATEGY[11]

When to Use This Procedure

For strategic planning affecting major changes, for community action, or for other types of accomplishments that require the coordination of a variety of persuasive efforts.

Materials Needed

1. Flip chart or chalkboard.
2. Markers or chalk.

How to Use This Procedure

1. The leader identifies the status-quo situation that is targeted for change or describes the current situation in contrast to the desired situation. The emphasis is on

---

[11]Based on "Force-Field Analysis: Individual Problem-Solving" in *A Handbook of Structured Experiences for Human Relations Training* (Vol. II, Rev.) (pp. 79-84) by J.W. Pfeiffer and J.E. Jones (Eds.), 1974, San Diego, CA: University Associates. For discussions of force-field analysis, see "Quasi-Stationary Social Equilibria and the Problem of Permanent Change" by K. Lewin in *The Planning of Change* (pp.235-238) by W.G. Bennis, K.D. Benne, and R. Chin (Eds.), 1969, New York: Holt, Rinehart and Winston, and "Kurt Lewin's 'Force Field Analysis'" by M.S. Spier in *The 1973 Annual Handbook for Group Facilitators* (pp. 111-113) by J.E. Jones and J.W. Pfeiffer (Eds.), 1973, San Diego, CA: University Associates.

description of the status quo (the current situation). The recorder draws a vertical line down the middle of the flip chart to represent the status quo. (See Figure 4.)

2. The group members brainstorm all of the forces that they see as working *against* the desired change in the status quo, i.e., all those forces that are holding the status quo in its current position and are in resistance to any of the forces for desired change. These forces are listed on the right-hand side of the chart with arrows pointing from right to left toward the status-quo line. (See Figure 4).

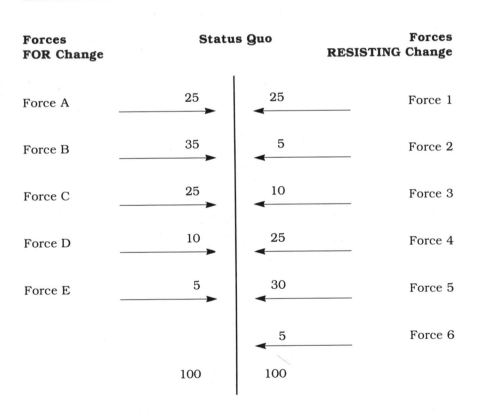

Figure 4. Illustration of Force-Field Strategy

3. When all of the forces resisting change in the status quo have been listed, the group weights each force in terms of its importance or strength by spreading one hundred points among the forces that have been listed.

4. The group lists all of the forces moving the status quo *toward* the desired change. These forces are listed on the left-hand side of the chart with arrows pointing toward the status-quo line.

5. When all of the forces moving toward change in the status quo have been listed, the group weights each force in terms of its importance or strength by spreading one hundred points among the forces that have been listed.

   Note: Steps 2 through 5 describe the field of forces that maintain the status quo. The group's strategic plan should focus on *diminishing resisting forces.* When resistance has been diminished, the current forces for change will be sufficient to move from the status quo toward the objective. (Experience indicates that this is the high-payoff strategy—the one that gets the greatest results with the least expenditure of resources.)

6. For each resisting force, the group lists the answers to the following questions. (It is important to be as specific as possible so that the effect of this analysis makes the "impossible forces" personal, tangible, and more accessible.)

   • What are the names of the people involved in this force of resistance?

   • What is the history of this resistance? How long has it been effective?

   • Where is this resistant force located? Does it have a specific geographical location?

   • In what ways or actions does this resistant force express itself?

   • What resources (money, equipment, materials, operational space, information, and distribution channels) are available to support this resistant force?

7. The group looks for specific actions that will reduce the resources listed in the previous step. For instance, members

may make comments such as "I have a friend who I think can change Max White's mind," "I know a way to quietly identify these 'ring leaders,' and I think this will cause most people to disassociate themselves from their cause," "I know one of their chief suppliers, and when he knows how the stuff is being used, I think he'll quit supplying them," or "Judy, Andrew, and Martha, who are in support of change, work in that same area; let's give them some exposure so that people will know that these few resisters don't represent the whole area."

8. *Optional:* The group may want to consider what it can do to increase the intensity of forces working *for* change. Experience indicates, however, that without deliberate efforts to diminish resistance, the more one pushes forces for change, the more likely one is to stimulate natural increases in resistance. This strategy is also a comparatively high-investment one: it usually requires much more time, energy, and other resources than simply trying to reduce existing resistance to the status quo.

GANTT PLANNING[12]

When to Use This Procedure

1. When planning projects (as opposed to scheduling ongoing processes);
2. When outlining the basic steps in a new plan and its areas of accountability.

Materials Needed

1. Flip chart.
2. Markers.
3. Index cards (3" × 5") or note pads and pencils for each member (optional—see Step 2).

How to Use This Procedure

1. The leader introduces the group to the project, its intended results or objectives, its deadlines, and its material constraints that the group should keep in mind during the planning.

---

[12]This activity and Figure 5, Illustration of Gantt Planning, are named after Henry Gantt (1861-1919), who introduced this particular process during World War I. For further information about Gantt's views, see *Gantt on Management* by A.W. Rathe (Ed.), 1961, New York: American Management Association.

2. *Alternative 1:* The group brainstorms a list of all of the steps necessary to achieve the project objectives.

   Alternative 2: The group follows the nominal group process by having the members work individually to list all of the steps necessary to achieve the project. When this has been done for three to four minutes, one member of the group presents his or her list on a flip chart. Others in the group add to that list any items that the first member did not include.

   Alternative 3: Individual members use 3″ × 5″ cards and write each step in the project on a separate card. After three to four minutes, one member of the group spreads his or her cards on a tabletop from left to right in rough sequential order. The other members then lay their similar cards on top of this first set and add, at the appropriate place in the sequence, any other steps they thought of.

3. On a clean sheet of newsprint, the recorder organizes steps or tasks thus far generated. Written from top to bottom according to the sequence in which the task will be done, these items form the vertical task analysis of a *Gantt chart* (see Figure 5).

4. A *time line* is drawn as the horizontal axis of the Gantt chart and is labeled for the relevant intervals of time (see Figure 5).

5. The group estimates how long each task will take and when each should begin and end; lines are drawn in the chart to express the duration of time estimated (see Figure 5).

6. The group determines who will be responsible for each task. This decision is designated by writing the person's name or representative legend on the task lines (see Figure 5).

7. The person responsible for each task submits an individual plan for the accomplishment of that task, including personnel, materials, budget, etc. These individual plans are presented and summarized for all of the tasks in a project budget. (This step may be done by individuals alone in preparation for a second meeting.)

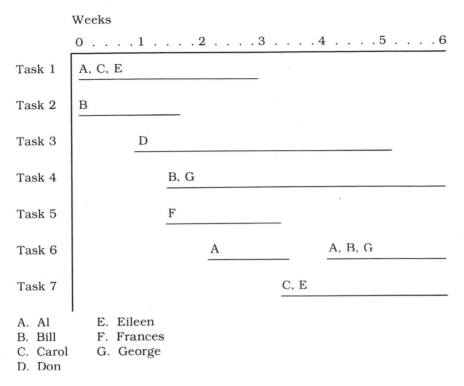

Weeks

| | 0 . . . .1 . . . .2 . . . .3 . . . .4 . . . .5 . . . .6 |

Task 1 — A, C, E

Task 2 — B

Task 3 — D

Task 4 — B, G

Task 5 — F

Task 6 — A   A, B, G

Task 7 — C, E

A. Al   E. Eileen
B. Bill   F. Frances
C. Carol   G. George
D. Don

Note: Task 1 begins on the first day of the first week and ends on the third day of the third week. Al, Carol, and Eileen will work exclusively on this step. Task 6 is done during the fourth week of the project by Al, then again during the last week when Al is joined by Bill and George.

Figure 5. Illustration of Gantt Planning

TEAM MAINTENANCE[13]

When to Use This Procedure

1. When you want the group members to begin thinking about the kinds of common problems they face;

2. When you want to focus the group's attention on self-maintenance, i.e., on issues concerning the dynamics and processes that cause the group to be less than fully effective.

Materials Needed

1. Flip chart.

2. Markers, one for each group member.

How to Use This Procedure

1. The members of the group brainstorm a list of problems that they think are probably being experienced by at least two people in the group. (For alternatives, see Notes 1 and 2 at the end of this activity.) The recorder charts all of these suggestions just as they are made. This brainstorming continues until everyone has made at least one contribution.

---

[13]This procedure is adapted from one learned while the author was studying under Charles A. Waters of Organization Dynamics, Inc., Berkeley, California.

2. The members of the group privately select the most significant and the second most significant problem named.

3. Using either a color-coding or a numbering system, the recorder charts on the brainstorming list how many of the problems receive a first selection and how many receive a second selection in terms of importance. When this has been done, the leader summarizes by isolating the one or two problems that seem to be rated by the group as the most important.

4. By consensus, the group selects one of the problems for immediate exploration.

5. The leader asks for illustrations of the selected problem. Each member is encouraged to share. The recorder charts all of these specific illustrations.

6. The group examines the list of specific illustrations and decides if one of those illustrations is especially representative of the problem, i.e., if solving that specific occurrence of the problem would also solve most of the occurrences.

7. If the problem selected in Step 6 is not stated in such a way as to allow working on its resolution, it is restated so that the group can (1) brainstorm its consequences and look for an alternative that eliminates these consequences and (2) brainstorm its causes and remove the causes.

Example:
Original Statement: "We need to redefine our roles."
Restated: "There is role confusion and the consequences are. . . ." (This statement allows the group to brainstorm the specific consequences, then work at redefining the roles to avoid these consequences.)

Example:
Original Statement: "We're still waiting for the personnel policy statement."
Restated: "What causes the delay in starting personnel policy?" (This statement allows the group to brainstorm the causes, then work at finding ways to eliminate these causes.)

8. When the problem is stated correctly, the group brainstorms for consequences or causes and then for possible solutions.

9. The group evaluates and chooses the solution or combination of solutions most worthy of implementation.

10. The group creates a specific action plan for implementation—designating who will do what and when.

11. The group reviews the other illustrations of the problem that were mentioned in Step 5 and eliminates any of these that will also be solved by the action plan.

12. Steps 6 through 10 are repeated until all of the illustrations mentioned in Step 5 have appropriate action plans.

13. If time permits, the leader returns to the list of problems in Step 1 and the group repeats the whole procedure. If time does not permit, the leader should schedule another meeting. (Once these problems have been recognized, they need to be solved or they will make more "noise" than usual in all the meetings that follow.)

14. The group forms an action plan, designating who will do what, when, where, and how. The leader has the group test this plan by asking, "How does this proposal differ from the status quo?"

Notes

1. The leader can "seed the clouds" for the brainstorming in Step 1 by charting or handing out this general list of potential problems:

   a. Goal setting and policy—products, services, customers, clients, investors, and employees:

      • Goals are not clear.
      • Goals are inappropriate.
      • Priorities are not clear.

- Goals are not being communicated and used constructively.
- Goals are not being met.

b. Resources—materials, equipment, space, and personnel:

- There are not enough resources.
- Resources are not provided in a timely fashion.
- Resources are inherently inadequate—flawed material, aged equipment, cramped or mislocated space, unskilled personnel.
- Resources are misallocated—not in line with goals and priorities.

c. Processes and procedures—the employment of resources:

- Procedures have not been designed.
- Procedures are not clear.
- Current procedures do not serve goals.
- Current procedures are inefficient.
- Current procedures conflict with each other.
- Procedures are not being followed.

d. Information and communications—organizational coordination:

- Important information is not available.
- Information is incomplete.
- Information is inaccurate.
- Information is not being given at a useful time.
- Information is not being given to the right people.
- Information is being given to the wrong people.
- Information is being ignored.
- Information is being misunderstood.

2. The leader can "seed the clouds" for the brainstorming in Step 1 by charting or handing out this general list of group maintenance problems:

a. Agenda:

- Agenda is not being announced ahead of time.
- Agenda is not announced early enough to allow preparation.

- Agenda is inappropriate—wrong issues.
- Agenda is not specific enough to allow preparation.
- Agenda is not being followed.
- Meetings are being called at the wrong time.
- Meetings are being held in the wrong place.
- Meetings are not long enough.
- Meetings are too long.

b. Group structure and attendance:
- The group is an ineffective size.
- The group does not include all the necessary people.
- The group includes some unnecessary people.
- Attendance of necessary people is irregular.
- The authority of the group is not well defined.
- Accountability for group action is not well defined.

c. Group member participation—behavior affecting group norm states:
- Some members do not seem as prepared as the group needs them to be.
- Some members of the group who want to participate cannot find "air time."
- Some members do not participate as much as the group needs them to.
- Some members do not express their information and opinions in a timely fashion, i.e., not to the whole group while the group is meeting.
- Some members are questioned more frequently than others.
- Some members are rarely questioned.
- Some members seem to be in frequent alliance against others.

d. Group process and procedure:
- The group operates without clearly defined procedures.
- The group uses procedures that are ineffective for its agenda.
- The group often works with a poor information base.

- The group spends little time analyzing or evaluating its information.
- Resolution is sometimes achieved autocratically or by pressure tactics of a minority.
- Sometimes the group's resolutions seem to be forgotten; nothing comes of them.
- The group rarely uses an effective memory system.

Part 3: Activities

⇨ 1: THE NEW MACHINE

Objective

In practice groups the participants reach a decision about which of three machines the Central Services Department will buy. Each practice group presents its final decision to the whole class with a brief justification for its decision.

Process Objectives

1. To be observed and coached by a teammate in practicing both *task* and *maintenance* skills.

2. To be observed and coached by a teammate in staying focused within the three stages of group process:
   - Building the information base;
   - Analyzing the information base;
   - Resolution—arriving at a group decision or common agreement about the meaning of the group's information.

Directions: Setting Up for Practice

1. The leader directs the class to pair off in teams of two.

2. The class forms practice groups of three pairs each (six people to a practice group).

3. Each team within the practice group chooses a letter: A, B, or C.

4. The members of each practice group seat themselves in two circles, according to the diagram in Figure 6, with everyone facing the center.

5. The leader hands out the appropriate team instruction sheet to each Team A, B, or C. Each team studies only its own instruction sheet and *does not read the others.* (Four minutes.)

6. The leader distributes an observation work sheet to each person, and everyone is given time to review it. (Two minutes.)

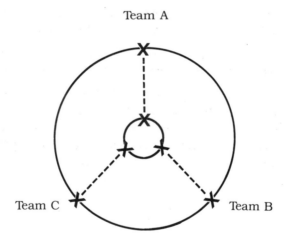

Figure 6. Practice Group Configuration

Directions: Practice in Stage 1, Building the Information Base

1. The members seated in the inner circle discuss the group's agenda. During this time, these three participants stay focused at Stage 1, building the information base. Seated behind them, other teammates observe the group's process as a whole and especially note the participation of their respective teammates, using the observation work sheet. (Three minutes.)

2. Teammates in the inner circle now turn to face those of the outer circle and discuss the observers' notes. (Two minutes.)

3. Teammates reverse roles and change chairs: the teammate who observed during Step 1 now becomes a group participant, and the other team member becomes an observer. The three new participants continue building the information base, as in Step 1. (Three minutes.)

4. Teammates once again face each other and discuss the observers' notes. (Two minutes.)

Directions: Practice in Stage 2, Analyzing the Information Base

1. Teammates again reverse roles. Inner-circle participants begin work on Stage 2, analyzing the information base. (Three minutes.)

2. Feedback as in Step 2 of Stage 1. (Two minutes.)

3. Teammates reverse roles and the participants continue the discussion from Step 1. (Three minutes.)

4. Feedback. (Two minutes.)

Directions: Practice in Stage 3, Resolution

1. Teammates reverse roles; participants begin work on Stage 3, resolution. (Three minutes.)

2. Feedback. (Two minutes.)

3. Teammates once again reverse roles. Participants complete Stage 3. (Three minutes.)

4. Feedback. (Two minutes.)

Directions: Summary

1. All members of each practice group discuss observations of their processes and one another's participation. (Five minutes.)

2. Each practice group chooses one of its members to report its decision to the rest of the class. Also, any worthy highlights of the group's process should be reported. (One minute.)

3. The class hears and discusses each group's decision and the highlights of the process.

THE NEW MACHINE
Observer Work Sheet

Directions: Each time your teammate speaks, make a tally mark in the chart below to show which kind of participation the person is providing. Then complete the respective section of this work sheet. You will be asked to share this information with your teammate immediately after you complete your three minutes of observation.

	Observation 1	Observation 2	Observation 3
Task Skills (used by my teammate)			
Initiating			
Providing information			
Asking for information			
Clarifying			
Elaborating			
Summarizing			
Compromising			
Maintenance Skills (used by my teammate)			
Gatekeeping			
Harmonizing			
Testing norm states			
Encouraging			

During Observation 1

Which of the following statements best describes the way my teammate participated as the group developed its information base?

_____ Reminded others to stay in Stage 1, building information

_____ Always stayed in Stage 1

_____ Jumped to Stage 2, analyzing the information base

_____ Jumped to Stage 3, resolution

During Observation 2

Which of the following statements best describes the way my teammate participated as the group analyzed its information base?

_____ Helped others stay in Stage 2, analyzing the information base

_____ Always stayed in Stage 2, analyzing the information base

_____ Had to go back to Stage 1, building the information base

_____ Jumped to Stage 3, resolution

During Observation 3

Which of the following statements best describes the way my
teammate participated as the group reached resolution?

_____ Helped others stay in Stage 3, resolution

_____ Always stayed in Stage 3, resolution

_____ Had to go back to Stage 2, analyzing the information base

_____ Had to go back to Stage 1, building the information base

THE NEW MACHINE
Team A Instruction Sheet

You may share this information during the group discussion *verbally only. Do not let the members of Teams B and C read this instruction sheet.*

You are Team A in the Central Services Department. Your function is to perform forecasting and cost analysis for small projects. This is done on a charge-back basis with the company's other departments, and you operate as your department's primary profit center.

You currently use the company's computer center (another department) to process your work. This means batching: you send work in by courier and wait at least two days for each turnaround. This slows down your production. It also discourages high-quality work. Your people would be more thorough in considering alternatives if they had hands-on computer assistance for manipulating cost variables and for predicting the consequences.

Teams B and C are in the same department with you. All of you are working successfully but are pushing the limits of your capacity. The department has generated $30,000 for capital and personnel investment during this next fiscal year.

For a minimal investment of $20,000, a minicomputer could be purchased that would provide all the features to speed work and allow thorough examinations of alternatives. This computer is effective because it is wholly designed for cost analysis. It does not have word-processing or accounting capacity.

Even considering the six-month installation and learning curve of the first year, with this minicomputer your staff could generate $25,000 of additional revenue for your department. In the second year, revenues would increase to $50,000. This revenue to the department should make it possible eventually for all teams to capitalize their improvement.

In addition to the revenue generated for your department, the improved quality and speed would probably help your company win an additional $250,000 in contracts in the first year and $500,000 in every year thereafter.

You have looked at the $14,000 terminal that ties your section into the company's mainframe computer. This would allow you to speed turnaround, but you would not get hands-on manipulation of cost variables without major reprogramming, estimated at a cost of $50,000 and a six-month delay. Even so, this terminal would give you half of the benefits for the first alternative.

With or without new equipment, you see no possibility of staff increase or reduction in your team during the next two years.

A representative from your team is going to attend a meeting with representatives from teams B and C. The purpose is to decide what equipment the department will buy this year.

Note: For this activity, rental or lease agreements are not to be considered.

THE NEW MACHINE
Team B Instruction Sheet

You may share this information during the group discussion *verbally only. Do not let the members of Teams A and C read this instruction sheet.*

You are Team B in the Central Services Department. Your function is to do budget analysis and cost control for your company. This is done on a charge-back basis with the company's other departments, and you operate as a profit center.

You currently use the company's computer center (another department) to process your work. You are limited to two monthly uses of computer time. This means batching: you send work in and wait two days for each turnaround. This slows production and keeps your people from effectively preventing budget variances.

In addition to your accounting staff, you have two typists.

Teams A and C are in the same department with you. All of you are working successfully but are pushing the limits of your capacity. The department has generated $30,000 for capital and personnel investment during this next fiscal year.

For a minimal investment of $14,000, the department could purchase a terminal that would tie you into the company's mainframe computer. This would give you the immediate access to the company's operational data necessary to prevent budget variances. This terminal would only serve for number crunching; it would provide no word processing. But, so far as you know, this terminal could be shared with Team A for its work in cost analysis and projections.

After six months for installation and training, your team would be able to save the company about $800,000 a year in budget variances. This would not increase revenue to the department, but it would greatly improve the department's service to the company as a whole. This, combined with whatever increased revenue might come from Team A's use of the terminal, should make it a good investment for both the department and the company.

You may have heard that Team A is looking at a minicomputer instead of this terminal. A minicomputer would not give your people the access to the company's mainframe computer that is so essential to preventing cost variances.

With or without the new terminal, you do not see any need for additional staff in your team this next year. But you are already "borrowing" typing help occasionally from Team C, and one year from now you will need to add a third typist at an estimated cost of about $15,000 per year.

A representative from your team is going to attend a meeting with representatives from Teams A and C. The purpose is to decide what equipment the department will buy this year.

Note: For this activity, rental or lease agreements are not to be considered.

THE NEW MACHINE
Team C Instruction Sheet

You may share this information during the group discussion *verbally only. Do not let the members of Teams A and B read this instruction sheet.*

You are Team C in the Central Services Department. Your function is typing proposals and billing clients for your company. This is done on a charge-back basis with the company's other departments, and you operate as a profit center.

Currently, you have three typists working on electric typewriters. They are working at maximum capacity. In an age of word processing, your people are severely handicapped. Revisions, attractive formatting, and graphic highlights are difficult to achieve; and given the time pressures, the company's proposals often look less professional than they should. It puts the company at a competitive disadvantage. Furthermore, there is little time for work on receivables. This is currently causing a cash-flow problem for the company.

Teams A and B are in the same department with you. All of you are working successfully but are pushing the limits of your capacity. The department has generated $30,000 for capital and personnel investment during this next fiscal year.

For a minimal investment of $10,000, the department could purchase a good word processor—one with all the bells and whistles necessary to make the company's proposals dazzle. And the unit is easy to use; all of your typists have operated a demonstration model and are dying to have units of their own. The vendor could make one or more of them available within one week of purchase.

Each word-processing unit would more than double the capacity of each typist. You think the department should buy two of them. This would allow you to transfer one of your typists to another department for an immediate savings of $15,000 this year. With the second unit you could take on all the work of one of Team B's two typists, saving another $15,000 during the year.

The word-processing units would also make time available for work on receivables. You could cut your average receivables time by thirty days—a one-time cash-flow savings of about $500,000 for the company.

Without the new equipment, you would have to add one more typist to your staff immediately, at an annual cost of $15,000. And you would surely need to add another a year later for at least another $15,000 per year.

You have heard that the other teams are looking at computer purchases. Could their acquisitions protect the department from your unavoidable costs?

A representative from your team is going to attend a meeting with representatives from Teams A and B. The purpose is to decide what equipment the department will buy this year.

Note: For this activity, rental or lease agreements are not to be considered.

2: CREATING AGENDAS

Objective

To review an agenda and suggest ways to improve it.
Practice groups redraft the agenda.

Process Objective

To practice publishing complete agendas. (See the check
list on page 14).

Directions

1. Alone, each class member reads the sample agenda
   (Figure 7) and identifies at least seven ways in which the
   agenda can be improved. (Four minutes.)

Memo From: Max
Date: June 18th
Subject: Monthly staff meeting, June 21st

Please be on time!

We have a lot to cover. RE: Summer schedule, and we'd like to get
things done quickly. See you there.

Figure 7. Sample Agenda

2. The class forms practice groups of three or four people each. Each group sits in a small circle.

3. In each group, the members share their suggestions for improvement.

4. Each practice group rewrites an improved form of the agenda.

5. The groups share their rewritten agendas with the class as a whole. These agendas are recorded on a flip chart.

3: STRUCTURING GROUP MEMBERSHIP

Objective

To determine the membership, leadership, and reporting relationships of a special task force. The task force's job will be to come up with a new product for the company to develop and sell.

Process Objective

To practice the principles of creating group structure:

- To keep the size of each group between five and nine members;
- To make sure the membership of each group represents the best possible combination of *available* human resources;
- To make sure the group has a competent leader who is appropriately linked to the organization's line-management structure.

Directions

1. The class forms groups of five to seven members each. Each group sits in a small circle.

2. Each practice group decides which of its members will serve on the task force. (Twelve minutes.)

Note: Each group may only choose members for the task force from its own membership or from people reporting (directly or indirectly) to its members. A group has reached resolution when it is prepared to report to the whole class on who the members of the task force will be, who its leader will be, and how the task force will be linked to the line-management structure of the organization.

3. One member of each group reports its resolution to the class as a whole.

4: INCLUSION ACTIVITY A

Objective

To include participants in the opening five to seven minutes of a meeting. The agenda is *changes in personnel and/or compensation policies that would contribute to increased organizational productivity.*

Process Objective

To practice inclusion in an activity. (See "Previews" on page 25).

Directions

1. Each class member works alone for two minutes to prepare for participation in the meeting.

2. The class forms practice groups of five to seven people each. Each group sits in a small circle.

3. The class leader appoints a leader for each practice group.

4. In each practice group, the leader:
   a. Opens the meeting with a brief statement of the agenda;
   b. Asks each member to take one minute to state his or her initial position with regard to the agenda;
   c. Briefly summarizes the members' initial positions and indicates what seems to be the appropriate place to begin in building the information base for the group's continued work.

5. Each practice group discusses in what ways this inclusion activity has assisted in controlling the group's norm state. (Six minutes.)

5: INCLUSION ACTIVITY B

This activity is to be performed by the same practice groups formed for Inclusion Activity A on page 77. It is conducted in the same way, with two changes:

1. Agenda: *what is the organization's greatest challenge in the next five years?*

2. The class leader appoints a new leader for each practice group.

6: MEMORY SYSTEMS

Objective

To generate three lists. Each list is to be made as long as possible in the allotted time (three minutes per list). List topics are:

1. The company's greatest strengths;

2. Characteristics of the company's best managers;

3. Ways for improving management communications.

Process Objective

To give each participant an opportunity to practice providing a group with a memory system. (See "Responsibility 5: Provide a Memory System" on page 17).

Directions

1. The class leader forms practice groups of three people each. The members of each group sit in a semicircle facing a flip chart and are given a felt-tip marker, masking tape, and wall space on which they can tape their completed newsprint charts.

2. In each practice group, each member takes a turn recording for the group as the group constructs the three lists described under "Objective" above (three minutes for

each topic). The member who is recording for the group should give special attention to that particular list with its topic heading.

3. During each three-minute period of constructing a list, each group strives for quality of ideas. It does not discuss or evaluate any of the ideas. The group helps the recorder to write down the members' *exact* words; the recorder is not permitted to substitute.

4. After each three-minute list-building period, each practice group scores each of its lists as follows:

Heading   +1 point

Items in List   +1 point/item

(The group deducts one point for every word that the recorder substituted for the actual words.)

7: BRAINSTORMING

Objective

To submit two ideas in a creativity contest. Your team is to come up with its most novel use for one Styrofoam cup.

Process Objective

To practice the brainstorming procedure. (See "Brainstorming" on page 29).

Directions

1. The class leader assembles practice groups of three to four people each. Each group sits in a semicircle facing a flip chart.
2. Each group appoints someone to record its ideas on the flip chart.
3. Each practice group generates ideas. (Three minutes.)
4. Each group evaluates its ideas and selects the two best ones. (Three minutes.)
5. The groups share their ideas with the class as a whole.

8: NOMINAL GROUP PROCESS

Objective

To come up with a suggestion about how brainstorming can be usefully applied in the company's meetings.

Process Objective

To practice the nominal group process. (See "Nominal Group Process" on page 31).

Directions

1. The leader forms practice groups of six to seven people each. Each group sits in a circle.

2. The groups each select a leader.

3. Each practice-group leader guides his or her group through nominal group process as the members explore the activity objective. (Twelve minutes.)

4. Each group leader reports his or her group's best application idea to the class as a whole.

9: MATRIX DECISION MAKING

Objective

To rethink the decision made earlier in Activity 1, The New Machine, on page 61.

Process Objective

To practice the matrix decision-making procedure. (See "Decision Matrix" on page 41).

Directions

1. Each class member rejoins the group of people with whom he or she previously worked on The New Machine. Each group sits in a semicircle facing a flip chart.

2. The groups each select a leader.

3. Each leader takes the group through a reconsideration of The New Machine decision it made earlier by following the matrix decision-making procedure. (Fifteen minutes.)

4. Each leader reports his or her group's decision to the class as a whole, displaying the matrix decision chart that the group produced.

10: FORCE-FIELD ANALYSIS

Objective

To engage in strategic planning for the company's affirmative action program. You are to submit an analysis of what you think are the most significant resisting forces in the organization and at least one suggestion for action toward diminishing each of these forces.

Process Objective

To practice force-field analysis. (See "Force-Field Strategy" on page 45).

Directions

1. The leader forms practice groups of five to seven people each. Each group sits in a semicircle facing a flip chart.

2. Each group selects a leader.

3. Each group's leader leads the group through its agenda according to the force-field strategy. (Twelve minutes.)

4. Each leader presents his or her group's analysis and action plan to the class as a whole.

11: GROUP GANTT PLANNING

Objective

To create a plan for a picnic. This picnic is a corporate community service provided for forty children from the city's home for the physically handicapped. The plan must take into consideration location, transportation, food and beverages, and group activity. The home's staff will participate to ensure adequate care for any special health problems that arise. The picnic, at the staff's request, should take place between 10:00 a.m. and 5:00 p.m. on any weekday (not Saturday or Sunday).

Process Objective

To practice the Gantt-planning procedure. (See "Gantt Planning" on page 49).

Directions

1. The leader forms practice groups of five to seven people each. Each group sits at a table with a flip chart at one end.

2. Each group selects a leader.

3. In each group the leader guides the group through its agenda, using the Gantt-planning process. (Twelve minutes.)

4. Each group's leader shares his or her group's plan with the class as a whole.

BIBLIOGRAPHY

Bales, R.F. (1950). A set of categories for the analysis of small group interaction. *American Sociological Review, 15,* 257-263.

Bales, R.F., & Strodtbeck, F.L. (1951). Phases in group problem solving. *Journal of Abnormal and Social Psychology, 46,* 485-495.

Barnlund, D.C. (1959). Comparative study of individual, majority, and group judgment. *Journal of Abnormal and Social Psychology, 58,* 55-60.

Benne, K., & Sheats, P. (1948). Functional roles of group members. *Journal of Social Issues, 2,* 42-47.

Cartwright, D., & Zander, A.F. (Eds.). (1968). *Group dynamics: Research and theory* (3rd ed.). Evanston, IL: Row Peterson.

Collins, B.E., & Guetzkow, H. (1964). *A social psychology of group processes for decision making.* New York: John Wiley.

Delbecq, A.L., & Van de Ven, A.H. (1971). A group process model for problem identification and program planning. *Journal of Applied Behavioral Science, 7,* 466-492.

Doyle, M., & Straus, D. (1984). *How to make meetings work: The new interaction method.* New York: Berkley.

Fisher, B.A. (1980). *Small group decision making* (2nd ed.). New York: McGraw-Hill.

Golembiewski, R.T. (1962). *The small group: An analysis of research concepts and operations.* Chicago: University of Chicago.

Hare, P.A., Borgatta, E.K., & Bales, R.F. (Eds.). (1965). *Small groups: Studies in social interaction* (rev. ed.). New York: Alfred A. Knopf.

Jones, S.E., Barnlund, D.C., & Haiman, F.S. (1980). *The dynamics of discussion: Communication in small groups* (2nd ed.). New York: Harper & Row.

Kepner, C.H., & Tregoe, B.B. (1965). *The rational manager.* New York: McGraw-Hill.

Lindzey, G., & Aronson, E. (1968). Group psychology and phenomena of interaction. In *The handbook of social psychology* (vol. 4, 2nd ed.). Reading, MA: Addison-Wesley.

McGrath, J.E., & Altman, I. (1966). *Small group research: A synthesis and critique of the field.* New York: Holt, Rinehart and Winston.

Pfeiffer, J.W., Jones, J.E., & Goodstein, L.D. (Eds.) (1972, 1973, 1974, 1975, 1976, 1977, 1978, 1979, 1980, 1981, 1982, 1983, 1984, 1985, 1986 . . .). The *Annual* Series for HRD practitioners. San Diego, CA: University Associates.

Pfeiffer, J.W., & Jones, J.E. (Eds.) (1969, 1970, 1971, 1973, 1975, 1977, 1979, 1981, 1983, 1985). *A handbook of structured experiences for human relations training* (vols. I-X). San Diego, CA: University Associates.

Shaw, M.E. (1976). *Group dynamics: The psychology of small group behavior* (2nd ed.). New York: McGraw-Hill.

Schein, E.H. (1969). *Process consultation: Its role in organization development.* Reading, MA: Addison-Wesley.

Ulschak, F.L., Nathanson, L, & Gillan, P.G. (1981). *Small group problem solving: An aid to organizational effectiveness. Reading, MA: Addison-Wesley.*